What's Different?

PHOTOGRAPHY
George Siede and Donna Preis

CONSULTANT
Istar Schwager, Ph.D.

Publications
International,
Ltd.

Right side up and upside down,
Someone's feet aren't on the ground!
Who is it?

Blow a kiss and
Break the spell.
Which frog's a prince?
Can you tell?

—— Let's play the What's Different Game. ——

—— Each row has one thing that's not the same. ——

—— Which one is it? What is its name? ——

What? You haven't played this game enough?

The question here is a bit more tough.

Now what's different in each row of stuff?

A tisket, a tasket!

Who's shopping with a basket?

Building blocks, windows, and game boards are square.

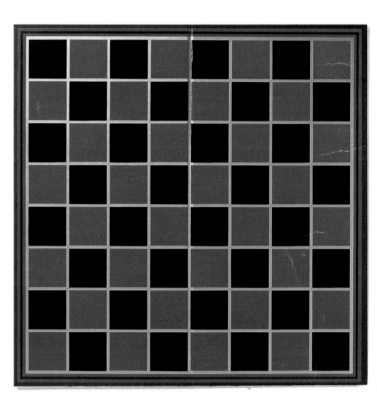

One shape is different. It can fly in the air. What is it?

Rub-a-dub-dub!
It's time for a scrub.
Which of these things
Don't belong in the tub?

Look! Kittens and mittens
    And bunnies and such.
But what do you see
    That's not soft to the touch?

Three things are in each row.

One thing doesn't go.

Can you tell? Do you know?

Take a look at these rows of three.

Look with care—what do you see?

One thing is different. Which would it be?

It's time for a snack,
    The food looks yummy.
Don't eat anything
    That's not for your tummy!

Feet on the Ground

How many children are wearing red shoes?

How many children are wearing blue shoes?

Name some times when your feet don't touch the ground.

Can you spot the twins?

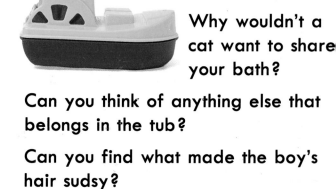

Fairy Tale Frogs

How many frogs are there?

There is a toad in the picture. Can you guess which one he is?

Can you find two matching frogs?

Do you know where frogs live?

Squares, Squares

How many squares are in the picture?

What are the names of the shapes inside the kite?

What is the name of the shape of the kite?

Scrub-a-Dub Tu

Why wouldn't a cat want to share your bath?

Can you think of anything else that belongs in the tub?

Can you find what made the boy's hair sudsy?